Paper, Metal
and Stitch

Paper, Metal and Stitch

Maggie Grey and Jane Wild

B T Batsford

Acknowledgements

We would like to thank our families for all their support, our friends for lending work, and Michael Wicks for wonderful photography. Finally, we would like to remember Jane's Mum Prue, and Louise.

First Published 2004
Reprinted 2004

Text and drawings © Maggie Grey and Jane Wild 2004

The right of Maggie Grey and Jane Wild to be identified as Authors of this work has been asserted by them in accordance with the Copyright, Designs and Patents Act 1988.

Volume © B T Batsford

ISBN 07134 8918 9

A CIP catalogue record for this book is available from the British Library.

Printed by Times Offset, Malaysia

for the publishers

B T Batsford
Chrysalis Books Group
The Chrysalis Building
Bramley Road
London W10 6SP

www.chrysalisbooks.co.uk

An imprint of **Chrysalis** Books Group plc

Photography by Michael Wicks (© B T Batsford)

Frontispiece
Ancient Emblems: 3 x 20 cm (12 x 8 in). A background of tea-dyed calico was built up with distressed Lokta paper and embossed metal shim. The metal was coloured with patination fluids and antiqued with black acrylic paint. Borders were made from stitched gold kid and metal shim with Lazertran transfers applied.

Contents

Introduction

Mixed media textiles are becoming very popular – increasingly so as stitchers see the wonderful results that can be obtained by using paper and metal in their work. Paper can be moulded, formed, cut, torn and stitched, and the techniques used in this book will enable large- or small-scale projects to be tackled with confidence. Metal adds a seductive gleam and new dimensions are explored using fine, soft, sheet metals, meshes, wires and coils.

This book will be of interest to all who work in the craft field. In it, we aim to lead the reader through the basic first steps to exciting ideas for combining techniques and using both paper and metal in new ways with a variety of media.

The materials used range from tomato purée tubes to brown paper, and very little specialist equipment is needed. Most will be found in your workroom – or kitchen!

Lots of new ideas and innovative methods will be found, from melting techniques for embossing powders to using paper with heat-reactive threads.

Using the book

The book is divided into two parts – Paper and Metal. The two parts follow a similar pattern, describing forming methods, ways of adding colour and texture and, finally, stitch. They are presented in a logical manner, enabling you to follow them through or to dip in and out as the fancy takes you. Most of the ideas can be intermixed and can be combined, bringing together paper and metal. Approach all the ideas with an open mind. Be willing to experiment and you will make many additional discoveries.

The methods described (for paper-making by Jane Wild, and for metal by Maggie Grey) work for us but are by no means the only approaches. Adapt them, extend them – and you'll not only find new ways but have a lot of fun.

Part One: Paper

1

Paper Textures

Paper is a natural material made from plant fibre. It is freely available and inexpensive. We use it every day, often without a second thought. Yet it is such a versatile medium and full of creative potential. Paper can be manipulated or moulded into any shape or form and assume any surface quality, it can be used successfully on a large or small scale, it may appear strong and sturdy or quite fragile. Machine-made and handmade papers provide a rich source of alternative surfaces for a variety of stitch techniques. Paper can also be used to enhance and embellish stitched items and, by experimenting with the following techniques, unique and exciting work can be created.

Purchased papers

Many unusual and exotic papers such as Lokta, Kozo and Japanese lace paper, are available from art, craft or specialist paper suppliers. These papers are often chosen for their unusual appearance or for particular surface qualities and, as many of them are surprisingly strong, they can withstand quite rough treatment. They are therefore ideal to use as surfaces for stitch. Everyday papers such as brown parcel paper (Kraft), water-colour paper, tissue, etc. are also full of potential and can be transformed with quite simple treatments.

A selection of purchased papers including Japanese lace paper, gold wrapping paper and Lokta embedded with skeleton leaves.

Opposite: Cas Holmes' *After the Rain* (detail) 200 x 160 cm (80 x 32 in). This piece contains blueprint fabric, layered papers, emulsion transfer, dye paste and stitch and is the artist's own technique. Inspired by the issues of flooding, it conveys how the beauty of water can hide hard truths about our perceptions of environmental conditions.

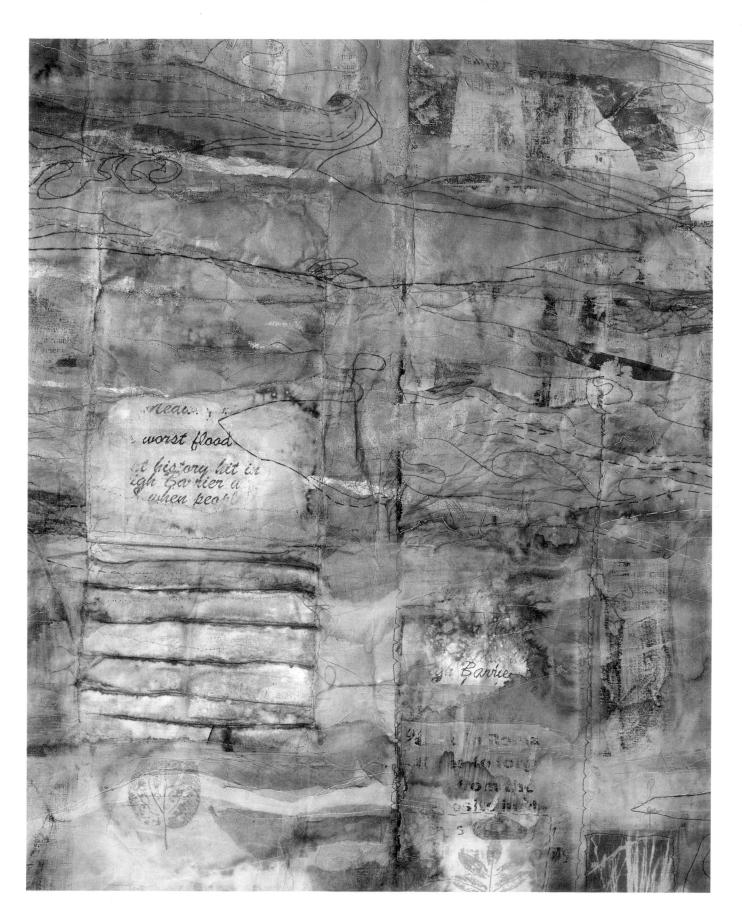

Cutting, tearing and burning

By cutting, tearing or burning paper, different edges can be created: soft, hard, wispy, ragged, etc. Experiment with the following ideas, compare the results and see how they work together. Sometimes the contrast of a cut edge against a torn or burnt one can be quite dramatic.

Paper has a grain and tears more easily in one direction. To see the difference, take a sheet of paper and tear a strip from side to side, then from top to bottom. The same applies if the paper is folded first and then torn along the fold, or torn against the edge of a ruler. Try this and the following suggestions with a variety of papers.

- Tear some paper towards you then away from you and see how the edges differ. The effect is more pronounced when one side of the paper is a different colour or printed
- Cut paper with as many different tools as you can, for example knives, pinking shears, nail or decorative scissors, or cut shapes with craft or stationery punches.
- Cut a shape (circle, square, etc.) in paper and then cut it into segments. Now tear the same shape and then tear that into segments. Arrange both shapes on a contrasting piece of paper and note the differences in character.
- Vary the manner in which you cut or tear: quickly, slowly, roughly. Try to control the paper or allow it to influence the outcome.
- Use a brush loaded with water to draw a line or shape on a piece of paper. Allow the water to soak into the fibres and then gently tear along the line. This method is useful if the paper is difficult to tear or you want more control over tearing.
- Hold a lighted incense stick against the edge of a piece of paper and, when it starts to smoulder, blow gently to control the burning. Press the burning tip of the incense stick against the paper to burn holes.

Any burning should be carried out safely. Work outside or in a well-ventilated room and have a container of water to hand in case anything catches fire.

Using an incense stick to burn holes in some Japanese lace paper.

Top: Cut and torn shapes were arranged on a strip of brown paper and applied by hand and machine. Below: Paper strips cut and torn to produce a variety of edges.

Opposite: An incense stick was used to burn edges and holes in various exotic papers. Gold leaf and inks were applied to some before they were burnt.

Crumpling and creasing paper

Simply crumpling or creasing a sheet of paper creates many surface patterns and textures. Repeatedly crumpling and creasing paper also softens the fibres, making it easier to stitch. Papers respond differently to crumpling. Some soften and others form hard creases, or tear. Experiment with as many papers as you can. Wet some paper before crumpling it and then manipulate it into a pleasing arrangement of folds and creases. Leave to dry and you will have a surface crying out for stitch, beads or other forms of embellishment.

Create a ruched effect by wrapping and crumpling paper around a plastic tube or plastic ruler. Place a piece of Lokta or another long-fibre paper in a bowl of water. Gently wring out and then wrap it loosely around a plastic tube. Scrunch the paper down gently but firmly to gather it up. Let it dry out completely – this may take a day or so – then carefully unwind the paper. It may feel as though it's stuck but just pull it slowly and steadily and it will unwind. Vary the effect with the following.

Ruching Paper

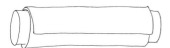

1. Damp paper rolled loosely around a plastic tube

2. Paper firmly scrunched

3. Unrolling the paper when it's dry

- Try other papers. Some may be more difficult to scrunch down and might need to be tied with string to prevent them unravelling.
- Vary the way you scrunch the paper.
- Try painting the paper with ink or dye before it dries.

Soak a piece of Lokta or Kozo in water, squeeze to remove excess water, gently crumple and then place on a waterproof surface. Dip your finger or a brush in some water and make small circular movements on the paper. This will distress the surface causing thin areas or holes and ridges to form. You can create highly textural and lacy effects and also manipulate or mould the paper while it's wet. You can also crumple a piece of damp Kozo repeatedly until it starts to weaken, then pull, gently teasing out the fibres. Some bits will break off with soft wispy edges.

4. A variation, paper scrunched in places

The arrows in this diagram represent the circular and rolling movements used to distress a piece of Lokta.

Ruched brown
paper and natural
Lokta overlaid with
coloured (ruched)
Lokta and a piece
of distressed Kozo.

Piercing paper

Paper can be pierced with almost any pointed instrument, and variations in the scale and density of the holes produced will create many different effects. Brown (Kraft) paper is a good first choice, but try other papers as well and experiment with the following.

- Place a sheet of paper, right side down, on a thick soft pad of felt or blanket, and pierce with various pointed instruments. Enlarge some holes by pushing a pencil through – this is particularly effective with painted or printed paper.
- Layer three or four pieces of paper on a soft pad and pierce the entire area fairly evenly with the point of a small skewer or a large needle. Concentrate the piercing in certain areas until the paper starts to tear and break up, then crumple and rub the layers together to encourage the distress. The layers can be applied to a backing as they are, or separated and used individually or to build up an area of texture.
- Try heavy piercing in straight lines, curves or isolated shapes for different effects.

Ideas for piercing paper.

- You can also use a sewing machine with an unthreaded needle to 'stitch' grids or random patterns. The machine can be set up for normal stitching or for free machining, whichever you prefer, and several layers can be stitched at one time. When the stitching is complete, remove the paper and separate any layers, then crumple and distress until you are happy with the result. You could also scorch the edges with an incense stick.

Above: this piece of bark was
the inspiration for several
experiments with pierced paper.

Experimental bark piece: 29 x
15 cm (11 x 6 in). Four layers of
brown (Kraft) paper, pierced,
distressed and torn were free
machined to a paper backing.
Highlights were added with
gilding wax and various threads
were twisted, wrapped with
enamelled wire and couched
into position.

Etched paper

Paper-Etch Dissolving Gel is a product that creates some exciting effects by carving into the surface of paper. It works by attacking cellulose fibres when heat is applied. The most dramatically carved effects are seen on very thick water-colour paper but, when used on less substantial paper, you can etch right through it. Paper-Etch can be applied straight from the bottle, used with a stencil, brushed or stamped on, but don't use a wooden print block as the gel will attack the wood.

Below left: Paper-Etch experiments on various papers including a tea-bag and paper decorated with ink.

Start with heavyweight smooth-surfaced water-colour paper. Rinse it under the tap for a minute or so to remove some of the size. When the paper is dry, draw a simple shape with Paper-Etch straight from the bottle, using varying amounts, and then put aside to dry. Place on a heat-resistant surface and zap with a heat tool, or cover with baking parchment and iron (don't use steam) until the treated area turns brown. Hold the paper under running water while you remove the brown area with a soft brush. When the paper is dry, you could apply more Paper-Etch to increase the effect. Also try the following.

Below right: Paper-Etch applied to paper (top); after heating with a heat tool (middle); scorched areas were removed and the surface inked to show the effect (bottom).

- Experiment with other papers. Remember that Paper-Etch will eat right through some papers, so make sure your designs or shapes will remain attached to the paper (think of stencil designs).
- Try it on the back of paper painted with acrylic paint – it removes the paper but not the paint.
- Paint the paper with water-colour paint, ink or very dilute acrylic paint before applying Paper-Etch.

Acrylic texture gels and gesso

There are many acrylic gels available containing added materials for creating different surface textures. These can be mixed with acrylic paint or painted at a later stage. By varying the method of application, many different effects can be achieved. The textures really come to life when painted and highlighted. Some texture gels may be too tough to stitch into, so you may wish to mask the areas to be stitched.

See how many effects you can create by applying texture gels or gesso with brushes, palette knives, rollers (brayer), sponges and print blocks – then experiment further.

- Make your own texture gels by adding different materials such as sand, sawdust, beads, etc. to an acrylic medium or PVA.
- Use the gel or gesso as an adhesive and adhere items to the surface.
- Apply a layer of texture gel or acrylic gesso and work into the surface with various mark-making tools. Paint the surface and, when dry, screw the paper up and distress it until the paper tears in places. Then place the paper right side down and brush with ink. It should seep into the cracks and creases.

Experimental samples, all painted with burnt umber acrylic and highlighted with gilding wax. Specific effects include: crushed sea shells in gesso, and scrim embedded in gesso. Pebeo mica mortar, garnet gel and gold mica medium (Golden products) were also used.

Puff paint

Puff paint coloured with a tiny amount of black acrylic paint then rubbed with gilding wax after heating. The samples include Puff paint applied with a roller then overprinted with a spiral print block and sprinkled with tiny beads (left), applied irregularly with card (top) and applied with a palette knife and drawn into with a shaper tool (below).

Puff paint is a binder that expands when heated. Subtle or flamboyant effects can be achieved depending on the method of application and the quantity used. It can be coloured before application with a little acrylic paint or coloured with various media after heating. Apply the puff paint, then place on a heat-resistant surface and heat straight away with a heat tool, taking care not to scorch it. Remove the puff paint from brushes, rollers, etc. with water immediately after use.

Apply puff paint using a variety of tools, such as rollers, print blocks, card, etc. and vary the quantity used. Perhaps drop small beads or glitter into it before heating.

Making your own paper

So far we have achieved some exciting results with purchased papers. However making your own paper is very satisfying and having an experimental approach to the process opens up many creative possibilities. The techniques we shall use do not require perfectly made paper – often less than perfect results and 'mistakes' have a special quality that can be quite inspirational. Japanese paper-makers believe that every sheet of handmade paper reflects the qualities of the maker. We shall look at paper-making in sufficient detail for the purposes of this book but, should you wish to experiment further, there are several excellent books available to borrow from a library or to buy (for details see Resources on page 126). Most of the materials and equipment required for paper-making are easy to obtain and inexpensive or can be adapted from everyday items.

Materials and equipment

Pulp: Cotton linters are part-processed cotton fibres in sheet form and are readily available from many art and craft suppliers. We shall assume they are used to make pulp. Other fibres can be used and the techniques will still work but the results might be different.

Bowl or bucket: You will need a waterproof container to soak the linters, and a sieve to strain the pulp.

Mould and deckle: The mould is a mesh-covered frame used to scoop up pulp from the vat. The deckle is an empty frame that sits on top of the mould and helps to keep the pulp in place and shape the edges of the paper. They are available in different sizes and can be obtained from various suppliers. An embroidery hoop can be used as an alternative. The Anchor 'Flexi-Hoop and Picture Frame' works well. Varnish the frame if it is wooden, stretch some mesh (such as net curtaining) taut in the frame, trim back the excess and it is ready to use. An empty hoop can be used as a deckle.

Aluminium mesh: Use a fine mesh of the sort used to repair car bodywork. It can be cut to the required size and shape and used without the support of a frame.

Blender: A domestic blender is used to beat the pre-soaked cotton linters to form the pulp.

Vat: This holds the pulp suspended in water. Any plastic container large enough to take the mould and deckle comfortably will do.

Felts: Wet-formed paper is transferred to a cloth or 'felt'. Use disposable kitchen cloths, sew-in interfacing, etc.

Pressing boards: You will need these to remove excess water from wet-formed paper. Any waterproof boards can be used.

Newspaper and old towels: Have a good supply to hand for mopping up. Paper-making is a very wet occupation!

Basic paper-making

1   Soak a small quantity of cotton linters in water for a few hours or overnight. Tear into small pieces, approximately 2.5 cm (1 in) square and place a small handful in the blender. Half-fill with water and operate in short bursts of about 15 to 20 seconds, resting between bursts. Five or six times should be sufficient to break down the linters. The pulp should be lump free and feel silky when ready.

2   Pay attention to your blender. Don't allow it to overheat. If the motor seems to be labouring, turn it off, remove some of the pulp and add a bit more water. You will get to know what suits your machine. Just proceed cautiously.

3   Half-fill the vat with water, warm or cold, and add some pulp, approximately one part pulp to four parts water. The consistency should be similar to pancake batter.

4   A couching mound makes it easier to transfer wet-formed paper from the mould. You can build one while the pulp is settling. Fold newspapers into small, medium and large rectangles and place them on top of each other starting with the smallest. Place a felt on top and moisten before use.

5   Stir the mixture in the vat to distribute the pulp, and hold the mould (and deckle) vertically over the vat. Then, in one continuous movement, lower the mould halfway into the vat, move it to a horizontal position and bring it up steadily, allowing the water to drain away for a few seconds. Gently agitate the mould to settle the fibres and remove the deckle if you are using one.

6   Hold the mould in front of you, with the pulp facing up. Then turn the mould through 90° and place the right-hand side of the mould onto the left-hand side of the mound (pulp facing the mound). Roll the mould onto the mound, press down

then roll off again. The sheet of wet-formed paper should be on the felt and the mould resting on its left-hand side. Cover with a felt and form the next sheet on top and continue in this way, adding more pulp to the vat as necessary. If at any stage you're unhappy with the results, float the pulp back into the vat and try again. To make thicker paper, either increase the quantity of pulp in the vat or layer two or more sheets of wet-formed paper.

7 To remove excess water, place some newspaper on the floor, then sandwich four to six sheets of wet-formed paper, interleaved with felts, between the pressing boards and stand on top of them. After pressing, leave the paper on the felt and hang it on a line to dry, or experiment with a bit of texture. When the paper is dry, it can be peeled off the felt.

Don't pour any pulp down the sink or drain; always strain the water from the vat before disposing of it.

Follow the guidelines to fold newspapers into small, medium and large rectangles

Form a mound by arranging them on top of each other starting with the smallest and cover with a 'felt'

Soak the linters

Process the linters into pulp in a blender

Add the pulp to the vat

Dip the mould into the vat

Scoop out some pulp on the mould

Place the mould on the mound.

Roll the mould onto the mound.

Deposit the pulp on the mound.

Cover with another felt.

Press the paper.

Dry the paper.

Texturing paper

Texture can be created and decorative elements added at various stages in the paper-making process. One of the simplest methods is to place a thick sheet of unpressed wet-formed paper (on a felt) on the mould or a piece of mesh, and drip or spray water onto the surface to make holes and craters. Allow the water to drain away and then peg up to dry. Try the same technique with a stencil or another form of mask.

Textured moulds for sheet-forming

The texture of a sheet of paper is partly determined by the mesh on which it is formed. A closely woven mesh produces a uniform sheet of paper. Experiment with different openweave fabrics and lace by stretching them in an embroidery hoop (see page 19) and using those as a mould. You can also use materials such as plastic mesh, lacy plastic table covering and bamboo table mats as alternative moulds without having to stretch them in a frame. These will all produce papers with different textures. You can form the sheet in the usual way but you may not be able to couch (transfer) it onto the mound – in which case leave it on the mould to dry then carefully peel it away.

Dip different items – wire shapes, skeleton leaves, lace, etc. – into the vat and they will get a covering of pulp.

A selection of materials used as
alternative moulds.

Textured paper formed
on alternative moulds.

Embossing

We use the term 'embossing' in this book to describe various techniques, including the use of embossing powders to produce relief designs on paper or metal.

Paper is embossed by impressing it with interesting objects or textured surfaces. Objects with well-defined surfaces and edges will produce the most accurate impressions but it is worth trying anything that appeals, for example leaves, grasses, shells, lace, stencils – the possibilities are endless. Use thick paper for embossing to prevent the object from tearing the surface – unless, of course, you fancy a distressed piece. Have plenty of pulp in the vat, make several sheets of thick paper and press them lightly. Leave the paper on the felt, place the objects on the paper and cover with another felt. If the objects are not too fragile, sandwich everything between two boards and stand on them or press firmly with your hands. Remove the objects and allow the paper to dry.

Try the following variations.

- Use a selection of objects such as kitchen utensils, DIY tools, springs, keys, etc. to texture the surface. Vary the way you impress the surface. Try pressing, pressing and twisting, hitting, or rolling the objects.
- Make shapes from wire or foamboard to emboss with and cover with a textured fabric rather than a felt, before pressing.
- Try embossing with textured and patterned rollers or print blocks. Indian wooden print blocks quite often stain the paper, which adds to the effect.

A selection of tools used for embossing paper and the resulting paper.

Embedded paper

When paper is embedded with decorative and textural material, the material is held in place by the fibres of the pulp, creating interesting effects and changing the surface quality of the paper. Snippets of thread or fabric, *pot pourri*, beads, sequins, seeds, etc. can be added to the vat. The resulting paper will contain these additions and every sheet formed will be unique. Another way of embedding additional material is to sandwich it between two sheets of wet-formed paper and then press the sheets together. You have more control over the position and quantity of material with this method, as the following suggestions illustrate.

- Experiment with different materials. For example, embedding wire or Wireform would enable you to bend and shape the paper.
- Embed various fabrics to reinforce the paper for stitch.
- Tear back part of the top sheet to reveal some of the embedded material.
- Try combining the techniques. For example, embed some paper with muslin (cheesecloth), emboss it and then manipulate into ridges, pleats, etc.

A detail from *Whispers* (page 51). Embedded Wireform in the pulp has created a strong and flexible surface.

2

Paper Shaping

Variations using the 'collagraph' mould (see page 32). Left: Heavy lace was torn and placed on the mould and pulp pressed on top to form a fragment. Middle: The mould was lined with Lokta tissue, the design free machined onto cold water-soluble film and placed on the tissue. Wet-formed paper was pressed firmly on top. Right: Fragment cast using pulp mixed with snippets of metallic fabrics, then painted with gesso.

Paper can be used with a variety of moulds. Using moulds for paper casting and *papier mâché* techniques enables basic structures or units to be repeated. As these can be varied at the moulding stage, it is possible to produce related rather than identical pieces. These can then undergo similar or different treatments, be integrated into one piece of work or form a series. The moulded paper is just the beginning.

Ready-made moulds for various crafts and baking purposes can be used, or you can make your own, which is fun and often produces unexpected results. Moulds can be built from scratch or taken from a master shape. Several materials and methods can be used, each with its own characteristics. Decorative frames or mouldings, found items, print blocks, etc. can be used as alternative moulds. The resulting shaped paper will be a negative impression of the original.

Making moulds

Polymer clay and Softsculpt (Formafoam) are versatile materials and simple or complex moulds can be made easily and fairly quickly. Both materials can be impressed and manipulated. The impressions can be used in a variety of ways: as individual moulds to produce small items for embellishment, or several impressions can be combined to form more complex moulds. Have a selection of objects to impress with, for example interesting buttons, jewellery, print blocks, moulding mats, shells, fossils, lace, ornaments, etc.

Polymer clay

Condition the clay well, either by rolling it in your hands or passing it through a pasta machine (which should not then be used for cooking) until it is soft and pliable. Roll out the clay – the size and thickness will depend on the object to be impressed. Dust both sides of the clay with cornflour (cornstarch) or talc to prevent it sticking to the mould or to your fingers. Press the object into the clay. If you want to increase the depth of the mould, gently push up the edges. Remove the object carefully, place the clay on a metal tray and bake according to the manufacturer's instructions. Then try the following variations.

- Roll out some polymer clay, cut or tear it into fragments and make random impressions from the same object. These can be rejoined or baked separately.
- Remove the object from the clay and then distort the impression slightly before baking.
- Take and bake an impression from a print block, tile or similar object. Then take an impression from this. Bake it and you have positive and negative moulds to use.

Above: A moulding mat and polymer clay impressions.

Below: Paper cast using the moulding mat and clay impressions. Background paper is decorated with Markal (Shiva) rubbings taken from moulding mat.

Softsculpt (Formafoam)

Softsculpt is thermoplastic foam available in thick and thin sheets; thick sheets are better suited to mould-making. It can be heated in an electric oven, with a heat tool or an iron, then quickly shaped around or impressed with an object. The results are not always predictable, but this adds to the appeal. If you're unhappy with any shape or impression, simply reheat and Softsculpt returns to its flat state. It retains heat for only a matter of seconds so it is important to have everything you require to hand. Cut some Softsculpt to size and heat, following the manufacturer's instructions, and then experiment with the following (note that there will be a difference in the depth and accuracy of the impressions).

Left: a Softsculpt (Formafoam) impression made with a button.
Top: a paper cast adhered to some epoxy putty (to add weight) and decorated with acrylic paint and Pearl Ex powders.
Right: pendants featuring similar paper casts combined with beads.

- Place an object on a firm surface, quickly cover with heated Softsculpt and press firmly with your hand until the impression is made.
- Repeat with another piece of Softsculpt but, this time, use a board to press down with.
- Another effect can be achieved by placing the object on a slightly textured surface.
- Place a piece of heated Softsculpt on a firm surface and impress with an object, then repeat with another piece of Softsculpt on a padded surface.

Fixing several related impressions to a firm sealed surface such as Medium Density Fibreboard (MDF) or plywood can make an interesting mould resembling a print block. Cut your chosen surface to the required size and arrange the impressions on it. Try several arrangements. Different effects will be achieved by butting the impressions together or spacing them apart. Remember that the mould is 'negative', so everything is in reverse. A gap between impressions will produce a ridge in cast paper. To fix the impressions to the background, apply PVA glue to both surfaces and leave for a few minutes until tacky. Arrange the impressions, cover with a board and clamp it in place. Leave for a few hours or overnight.

Left: A complex Softsculpt (Formafoam) mould made with impressions taken from a small clay head and a chess piece from a casting kit. The resulting cast was created using wet-formed paper.

Below left: A mould for casting a frame, the raised section in the centre produces a recess.
Below middle: A frame cast, using wet-formed paper, was painted with gold acrylic then Liming wax (a Liberon product) applied and partially removed with clear wax. The recess can be seen in this example.
Below right: Pulp containing snippets of fabric was used to cast a fragmented frame. Burnt umber acrylic was diluted and allowed to trickle over a base of acrylic interference colours. Impressed pulp forms the insert.

Quite complex moulds can be built using this technique. By alternating textured, patterned and plain areas or varying the depth of the Softsculpt components, it is possible to create moulds designed to frame or provide areas to incorporate stitched or mixed media pieces.

Making a Softsculpt vessel:

To make three-dimensional moulds with Softsculpt, choose simply shaped objects that you can encompass easily with both hands. For example, to make a mould for a vessel, select a suitable object, cut a piece of Softsculpt large enough to cover it, heat in the oven and place over the object, wrap your hands around it and press. Remove the Softsculpt from the object. The edges will be fairly ragged but these can be trimmed back to give a neat edge, or you may like to leave some of the folds and creases and just snip into parts of the edge.

1. Mould heated Softsculpt (Formafoam) around a small vessel

Once you have a three-dimensional mould it is possible to insert small pieces of impressed Softsculpt. Remember that you are working in reverse, so the impressed shape will produce a raised effect on the finished item. Place the impressed Softsculpt face down on the outside of the mould and carefully cut around it. Remove the cut-out, then brush the edges of the hole and the impressed Softsculpt with a little PVA glue. Leave for a few minutes until the glue is tacky and then insert the impressed Softsculpt and press into place. It will probably not be a particularly neat fit but, as long as it is secure, it will hold up during use.

2. Make several impressions and cut them out

3. Cut holes in the Softsculpt using the impressions as a guide

When you have made and used a three-dimensional mould, it is easier to see the potential in different objects. For example, try moulding around a ball of string or some fabric that has been screwed up tight and wrapped with knotted threads. Alternatively, look at the various seed pods and other botanical products available from florist and craft suppliers.

4. Fix the impressions in place with PVA

Far left: A piece of Friendly Plastic was heated and impressed then embedded in 'No More Nails' to form a small low-relief mould.
Centre: A latex mould was made.
Left: By using both moulds, positive and negative paper casts were made.

'Collagraph' method

The plates used for collagraph prints are made by gluing a variety of textural materials to heavy-duty card. We can adapt this technique to produce low- to high-relief moulds, on surfaces such as medium-density fibreboard (MDF), plywood or suitable objects such as plates, bowls, frames, etc. You may already have made a collagraph plate, in which case thoroughly seal all sides with varnish before using it as a mould.

Opposite: A vessel was cast in three-dimensional Softsculpt (Formafoam) mould. Covered with gold leaf and painted with black spirit-soluble dye then sponged with methylated spirit.

Making a 'collagraph'

Before you start, consider the following.

The cast paper will be a negative impression of the mould, so a mirror image of any design should be transferred to the MDF, etc. If you want to create a raised area in the cast, it must be recessed in the mould and vice versa.

Don't create undercut areas, when building up or carving into a surface. Keep the edges straight in a U shape or a V shape, otherwise paper may get pushed under the surface of the mould and tear when you remove it.

U-shaped and V-shaped grooves in cross-section.

Make sure that everything is sealed with two or more coats of waterproof varnish, to prevent water seeping in and spoiling the mould.

- Start with a small piece of MDF or plywood and have a selection of interesting materials to hand, for example card, textured papers and fabrics, string, skeleton leaves, etc. Use PVA or an acrylic medium as an adhesive and build up a low relief pattern or design with some of your materials. Leave for 24 hours or until the adhesive is dry and then seal with varnish. Alternatively …
- Cover your surface (MDF, etc.) with a thick layer of acrylic modelling paste or a DIY adhesive such as 'No More Nails'. Build up a design by drawing into the paste with any mark-making tools, impressing the surface or embedding items. When satisfied with your design, leave it to set. This may take a few days if the paste is thick. Seal with varnish.

Undercut grooves in cross-section: paper will get trapped and may tear.

- Tear different sizes of strips and shapes from thick blotting paper, coat them generously with acrylic gel medium and start to layer them onto your chosen surface. Work intuitively, building up interesting shapes and patterns or follow a simple design. As the gel soaks in, the blotting paper becomes quite soft and you can work into the surface with a stick or similar tool for details. When set, seal with varnish.

Making a 'collagraph' mould. Top left: The design drawn and the main areas defined with torn blotting paper. Top right: Building up the background. Below left: The mould, finished and sealed. Below right: The resulting paper cast, the recessed areas of the mould produce the raised areas in the cast.

Making a master shape

Master shapes or forms can be modelled in clay, polymer clay and plasticine, or constructed with any materials that can be shaped and fixed into the desired form. Flexible or rigid moulds can be taken from the master and it can also be used as a mould for *papier mâché* techniques.

For example, the master for a vessel can be constructed from corrugated paper cut to the height of the vessel plus roughly 5 cm (2 in), rolled to the diameter of the base and taped securely. More corrugated paper can be added to the roll to form a basic structure, which can be refined by adding a combination of paper and various acrylic gels, heavy body medium, gesso, etc. A form constructed in this way will have to be completed in stages to allow time for the acrylic gels to harden. Texture and relief patterns can be added to the surface by applying papers, fabric, found items, texture gels, dimensional paints, etc. Seal with two or three coats of varnish.

1. Basic shape formed with rolled corrugated card

2. Shape refined with paper and acrylic modelling paste

3. Torn photocopies arranged as a basis for a relief design

4. Design shapes simplified and built up with blotting paper and acrylic heavy gel medium

5. Texture created with tissue paper and heavy gel medium and detail added with relief outliner

Latex rubber

Opposite: A cameo (top) was used to make the Mold 'n' Pour mould (right). The casts were made with wet formed paper and one (below) was covered with gold leaf and painted with brown spirit-soluble dye and methylated spirits.

Below: A fragmented vessel was cast with pulp containing snippets of fabric using the latex mould (in the background beside the master form). The vessel was decorated with cheat's verdigris (page 45). Copper wax and turquoise paint were used and 'knocked back' with black patinating wax.

Latex liquid rubber is an emulsion which air-dries on the surface of a master shape and forms a rubber skin that is extremely flexible. Two mould-making techniques can be used, 'dipping' and 'paint on'.

Dipping is the best method for masters made from porous materials such as plaster of Paris, fired clay or wood. Generally speaking, the master is dipped into the latex for a few seconds, removed and any air bubbles burst, then re-dipped for 15–20 minutes, removed and left to cure overnight. Dust the mould with talc before peeling it from the master, to prevent sticking.

For masters made from non-porous materials, the paint-on method is better. Several layers are painted on with a soft brush, being allowed to part-cure between applications. As many as 8 to 15 layers may be needed depending on the size of the master. Muslin (cheesecloth) can be sandwiched between the layers to strengthen the mould. Cure and release as above.

Mold 'n' Pour

A product called Mold 'n' Pour is ideal for making small, flexible moulds. The pack contains a blue and a white compound. Knead equal quantities of these until the colours blend, then place on a flat surface and impress with an object. Wait for about ten minutes, then remove the object and the mould is ready to use.

Alternative moulds

Print blocks, especially some of the large ones, can be used as moulds, and interesting effects can be achieved by combining printing and casting from the same print block. Positive and negative aspects of design can be explored. Other objects can be used as paper casting and *papier mâché* moulds: plastic packaging, basketwork, stones, stone mouldings, decorative wrought iron, trees, etc.

Using the Moulds

Paper casting

Compressing pulp or wet-formed paper into a mould forms a paper cast. Both methods produce a cast with good detail, although surface quality differs. A cast made using the pulp method has a slight additional texture to it. Paper shrinks as it dries so it is better to cast around the inside surfaces of an object or mould to prevent cracking. Paper should release easily from flexible moulds or those with a shiny surface but, if in doubt, use petroleum jelly or silicon spray as a release agent.

The same mould was used to make casts from wet-formed paper (left) and pulp (right); both casts were painted with burnt umber and bronze acrylic.

Combining techniques

Four stages showing the development of decorated brown paper; the materials are listed in order of use.
Left: Markal (Shiva) paintstick and black ink. Bondaweb (fusible webbing), coloured with metallic paint and ironed. Embossing powder. More embossing powder and black ink.
Middle: Metallic and glitter wax crayon, black and brown ink. Painted Bondaweb, zapped with a heat tool. Embossing powder. More embossing powder, gilding wax and Pearl Ex.
Right: Glitter wax crayons and blue ink. Coloured Bondaweb (fusible webbing), ironed. Another layer of Bondaweb, ironed and worked into with Markal paintsticks. Zapped with a heat tool and rubbed with gilding wax.

Thoroughly crumple a piece of brown paper, scribble on it randomly with metallic oil or wax crayons and then brush with ink. Leave to dry. Peel the backing from some painted or unpainted Bondaweb (fusible webbing) and drape it over the paper. Zap with a heat tool or cover with baking parchment and hover an iron over the top to melt the webbing onto the paper without flattening it. Sprinkle some embossing powder onto the melted webbing and heat. Apply transfer foil or work into the surface with metallic Markal (Shiva) paintsticks or try a combination. Brush with more ink or paint and keep going until you're happy with the effect.

Colour some Japanese lace paper with metallic Markal (Shiva) paintsticks and leave for about 48 hours to dry. Tear about four pieces roughly the same size, layer and stick them together with diluted PVA then manipulate into a pleasing shape and leave to dry. Or tear the lace paper into small pieces and use to make a *papier mâché* object. You can use a small butane-fuelled blowtorch (the type used in the kitchen) to scorch and distress the paper. Work outside over a bowl of water, light the blowtorch and hold the paper with pliers. Gently play the flame over the surface. It will start to buckle and scorch. By allowing the paper to ignite then blowing out the flame repeatedly, you can slowly burn holes and edges. Drop the paper in the water if you're unable to extinguish the flame.

Draw a pattern or design on paper with PVA glue and allow to dry. Paint the surface with coloured ink (not acrylic) or water-colour paint. Brush some areas with Pebeo Mica Mortar when the ink has dried and then follow with a coat of black ink (not acrylic). Use a brush or sponge to apply a little household bleach, diluted with water, to lighten and texture some areas. The final touch is to add highlights with transfer foil. Breathe on the PVA to activate it, place the foil shiny side up on the glue and rub, adding a little at a time.

Japanese lace papers, coloured with metallic Markal (Shiva) paintsticks, layered and moulded then scorched with a domestic blow torch. Moulds include a large foam print block (top middle) and a mask-making mould.

A design: 52 x 34 cm (20 x 14 in), worked in PVA glue and decorated with inks, Pebeo mica mortar, bleach and transfer foil.

4
Into Stitch with Paper

As we have seen, paper is an exciting and versatile medium. Many shapes and surfaces can be created and materials such as fabric, metal, plastic, etc. can be combined successfully with paper or paper objects. Stitch can be added in a variety of ways. It may be functional, forming part of the structure, linking both visually and physically, finishing edges, etc. It may also be used to enhance by adding texture, pattern and colour or to secure other items.

Time Passes: 90 x 38 cm (36 x 15 in). In this delightfully distressed work, calligrapher Elizabeth Forrest has covered string and knots with paper pulp. This enhances the calligraphy on smooth, hand-made paper.

Approach stitch flexibly. Consider simple stitches as a means of mark making, stitching before painting and decorating the surface, embedding stitch in the paper as you make it or experimenting with a favourite technique to see if it can be adapted.

We use the term 'patch' in both parts of the book to describe any shaped piece of paper, metal, etc. that is applied to another surface. In most cases, the patches are constructed, stitched or decorated prior to application.

Reinforcing paper for stitch

Paper doesn't have to be reinforced but using a stabiliser or backing will strengthen it, help prevent stitches pulling through or tearing the surface and add weight to fragile or lightweight papers. Reinforce paper with a stabiliser such as iron-on interfacing, which is available in several weights and easily applied. Alternatively, use Bondaweb (fusible webbing) to bond paper to various materials. Bonded paper can look flattened but this can be overcome by crumpling the paper before bonding, not applying too much pressure with the iron, or crumpling and distressing it after bonding. An alternative is simply to back the paper with felt, sew-in interfacing, etc. without bonding it in place.

Select one type of paper and experiment with different backings, interfacing, fabric, metal shim, etc. to see how the handle of the paper is affected.

You can also strengthen paper as you make it by sandwiching fabric, Wireform, etc. between sheets of wet-formed paper.

Papers such as Japanese lace paper can be strengthened with a coat of acrylic varnish without clogging up the holes, so the paper can be caught down using stab stitches. Lay the paper on baking parchment or waxed paper and brush on the varnish, using the matt finish unless you want shiny paper.

Whispers: 18 x 17 cm (7 x 6 in), areas of a Softsculpt (Formafoam) mould were covered with layers of wet-formed paper. Torn Wireform was dipped in the vat for a covering of pulp, placed on the mould and more pulp pressed on top. When dry, the Wireform was flexed to lift parts of the cast. A few hand stitches were added and gesso applied followed by a coat of blue acrylic and finally gold acrylic and burnt umber glaze.

Stitching by hand

Simple stitches can be used to great effect, adding emphasis rather than overwhelming paper surfaces. The best way to explore the combination of paper and stitch is to work a few samplers using a variety of threads and paper surfaces. To begin with, experiment with stitches such as straight, running, chain, cross, buttonhole and fly. Vary the size and style of the stitch: regular, irregular, loose, etc. Apply gesso, texture gel and emulsion or acrylic paint to one of your samplers, including the stitches. Then highlight some areas of stitch with gilding wax.

Cut or tear several paper patches, varying the size but keeping to the same shape. Then apply them to a paper background by stitching around the edges, through the shapes or by holding them in place with a single stitch.

Hand stitches

Straight Stitch

Running and Whipped Running Stitch

Cross Stitch

Buttonhole Stitch

Chain and Detached Chain

Fly Stitch

Applied stitch

Stitching into a paper surface is not always practical. It may be too tough or you may want the stitch element to be visible from one side only. In either case, another ground can be stitched and then applied to the surface with an acrylic medium or PVA. Almost any fabric can be used, adding texture and stitch to the surface and then being painted or not, depending on the desired effect.

Stitching with the machine

With the machine set for normal stitching (feed dogs up) and some of the paper reinforced with interfacing (sew-in or iron-on), try the following.

- Stitch a series of lines in straight stitch or zigzag, or use built-in stitch patterns if you have them. Vary the size of the stitch and the distance between the stitches. Crumple the paper first and see if that makes a difference.
- Tear or cut a patch and apply it to a piece of paper, using one of the stitches from your experiments.
- Use the built-in stitch patterns to stitch strips or shapes on paper (without a support), then tear along the stitches to form braids and patches.

Set the machine for free machining by fitting an embroidery foot, dropping the feed dogs and adjusting the thread tension if necessary. In general, paper won't need to be framed for free machining. Select a piece of reinforced paper and stitch straight or curving lines to get the feel of it. Stitch at a comfortable speed and avoid jerky movements. If you overstitch an area, the paper will tear.

From a selection of decorated papers, tear or cut patches in different sizes and shapes and arrange them on a larger piece of reinforced paper. A tiny spot of PVA will hold them in place.

Left: Decorated papers wrapped with chenille.
Middle: A piece of woven paper dipped in wax and covered with bronze powder was attached to the background with one large detached chain stitch. Detached chain was also used to attach small paper patches decorated with gold leaf and spirit-soluble dye.
Right: Various papers were layered in this sample, including cartridge (construction) paper decorated with gesso and gold acrylic then distressed and inked. Running stitch was used to apply and link the paper elements.

Ideas for applying patches
by machine

There are several options now. The shapes can be outlined or blended into the background with stitch or secured with stitched lines, patterns or motifs.

Softsculpt (Formafoam) impressed with a lace flower was used to cast several fragments. The fragments were coloured with gilding wax and ink then free machined to paper backgrounds.

When applying cast paper fragments to another surface, you may want to blend the edges. This can be achieved with dense free machining between the fragment and the surface, although it may distress the fragment. Another method is to cover the fragment and part of the surface with a loosely woven fabric, manipulate the weave until most of the fragment is visible (but the edges are all or partly obscured), then free machine to blend. A mixture of hand and machine stitch is another option.

Links

Hand-stitched links

Link separate units or fragments of paper/cast paper with variations of lacing or insertion stitches. The fragments or units are likely to have uneven edges and surfaces, so allow the pieces to sit comfortably, adjusting the distance between the edges and the stitch tension as you work. Piercing holes in the edge prior to stitching can make the process easier, particularly if you are working with fiddly or unwieldy pieces.

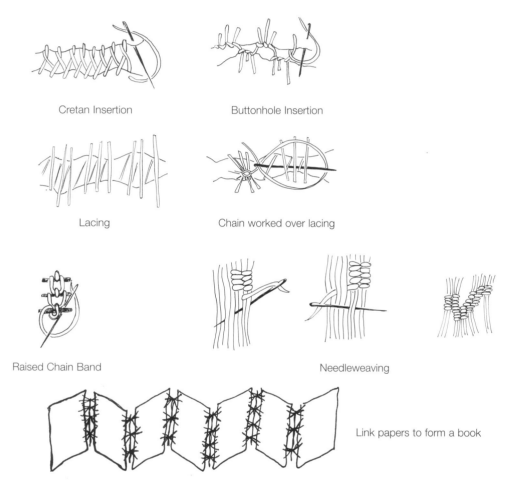

Cretan Insertion

Buttonhole Insertion

Lacing

Chain worked over lacing

Raised Chain Band

Needleweaving

Link papers to form a book

Three cast paper fragments, formed on a Softsculpt (Formafoam) mould, were linked with insertion stitches and embellished with needle weaving, bullion stitches and beads.

Link small patches to form borders

Fragment inserted in a frame

Experiment with shapes and
positions in frames

Machine-stitched links

A heat-activated stabiliser or vanishing muslin, such as Thermogauze, is useful if you are linking or inserting fragments with free machining. When Thermogauze is subjected to heat from a heat tool or an iron, it disintegrates. If the paper is flimsy, fit the Thermogauze in a frame, turn the frame upside down and attach paper patches with temporary adhesive or pins. Free machine between the edges of the paper. Remove from the frame and place on a heat-resistant surface. Then zap both sides with a heat tool until the Thermogauze turns brown and can be brushed away.

Another fabric to consider is Kunin, which is acrylic felt. When zapped with a heat tool, the surface distorts and partly disintegrates. Interesting effects are possible as remnants of the felt remain around the stitching and the paper will probably distort. Pin some paper patches to the felt and free machine between the edges. Then place felt side uppermost on a heat-resistant surface and use a heat tool cautiously. The felt will start to distort and holes will appear. Turn it over to check progress. Continue until you're happy with the result. You may find that you prefer the wrong side. It is advisable to work a test piece, as some colours react differently.

When using either of these fabrics experiment with the manner of stitching. For example:

- Stitch from edge to edge in a gently curving manner or with an angular zigzag. Then stitch across the linking stitches.
- Stitch from side to side continuously or in blocks of stitch, varying the density of stitch.

To insert a patch or fragment, cut or tear a paper frame large enough to encompass the fragment and allow for a gap. Fix both pieces to Kunin (acrylic) felt or Thermogauze and join with free machining. Take the stitches right into the frame and, if the fragment has a motif or design, try to echo the shape with the stitching. Remove the Kunin or Thermogauze as described above.

Right: Thick paper patches applied to Kunin (acrylic) felt using a built-in stitch. After zapping the felt some distortion can be seen.
Far right: Various papers applied to Kunin felt with free machining and a built-in stitch. More distortion can be seen after zapping this sample.

Crumpled and decorated brown (Kraft) paper, torn to form a frame, and small paper casts made using a moulding mat were pinned to a piece of Thermogauze. They were linked with free machining and the Thermogauze removed with a heat tool.

Structural links

By embedding threads between two sheets of wet-formed paper, you can link the paper as you make it or lay down the foundations for linking at a later stage. For example, make four sheets of paper and transfer two of them to a smooth or textured surface, leaving a gap in between. Cover both sheets of paper and the gap with several lengths of thread, string, etc. Place the remaining two sheets of paper on top, cover with a felt and press with a roller. Paper can be linked vertically, horizontally or diagonally into any arrangement using this technique.

The threads could form the foundation for composite stitches such as raised chain band, or for needle-weaving.

A variation is to trickle a thread backwards and forwards across the paper, extending over the edges on opposite sides so that loops are formed. Cover with another sheet of paper and press as before. Several sheets of looped paper can then be laced together.

Yarn or wire sandwiched between two sheets of wet formed paper to link several sheets together

Laced links

Wrapped and woven links

A book created with paper cast on small slate tiles and linked with continuous threads. The linking threads were buttonholed and running stitch worked. The entire surface was sealed with gesso then coloured with bright metallic paints. When dry, a coat of Liming wax (a Liberon product) was applied and then partially removed with clear wax.

Reflections: 101 x 64 cm (40 x 25 in), inspired by Louise Bourgeois' installation 'Toi et Moi'. A sheet of MDF was cut into sections and a mould built up with blotting paper. The cast was made using wet-formed paper and was removed from the mould while still damp so it would distort as it dried. The sections were laced together and the cast was painted with gesso with highlights in white gold leaf added.

Fusible thread and soluble film

Highly textured patches can be made using a combination of paper, fusible thread and soluble film. The patches can be used separately or joined together.

Frame wrapped with fusible thread

Torn paper placed over the fusible thread

Paper covered with cold water soluble film and free machined

Wrap a small frame quite densely from top to bottom then from side to side with Grilon or YLI fusible thread. Arrange a selection of torn papers on the frame. Cover with a piece of lightweight water-soluble film and tack or pin it in position. Set your machine for free machining, with fusible thread on the bobbin and a metallic thread on top. Stitch around the inside of the frame to begin with, then stitch within the frame, following the outline of the papers or doodling. Alternatively, you could draw a simple shape, pattern or design on the soluble film and stitch the outlines. Vary the density of stitch, leaving some areas unstitched to increase the distortion. Cut the threads and remove the patch from the frame. Fill a small container with hot water (just bearable) and immerse the patch. Allow it to shrivel up then remove it from the water. Squeeze out the excess water and leave to dry. The water temperature is fairly critical. If it is too hot, the fusible thread disintegrates; if it is not hot enough there is little distortion. Experiment with different papers and paper thread, woven or layered paper and different stitch patterns.

Fusible thread samples including:
Top left: A hexagonal frame was wrapped with fusible thread and a hexagonal spiral stitched heavily on the soluble film and paper.
Top middle: A design was drawn onto soluble film, torn papers were arranged fairly carefully and the main lines stitched. Although distorted the design can be seen.

Cold water soluble film

Using lightweight cold water soluble film as a support for hand or machine stitch enables you to combine it with wet-formed paper or pulp, which will dissolve the film and leave the stitch element embedded in the paper. This technique can vary, so adopt an experimental approach – it will be well worthwhile. A variety of stitch effects can be created and additional material (fabric snippets, beads, etc.) can be added. A sticky residue is formed when the film dissolves, so check that the paper doesn't stick to the mould, felt, etc.

Start with a simple experiment. Set your machine for free machining and frame-up the soluble fabric. Cut several lengths of heavy metallic thread, form a grid on the soluble film and couch using a free zigzag. Change to a straight stitch and work a few diagonals or fill in some of the squares. Remove the film from the frame, trim any excess and experiment with the following ideas.

- Sandwich the film between two thin sheets of wet-formed paper and press. Tear some of the paper away to reveal the stitch.
- Apply a release agent, line a mould with Mulberry or Lokta tissue and cover the film with wet-formed paper or pulp. The tissue can be distressed and partly removed with a wet brush (see page 26).
- Place the film on a piece of mesh and drop the pulp on top, partly covering the stitch.
- Combine hand and machine stitch on the soluble film and/or apply snippets of fabric, beads, sequins etc.

Rectangles of copper shim were machine stitched together using cold water soluble film as a support. The film was placed on a piece of mesh and partly covered with pulp. When dry, copper wire and pierced, waxed brown paper were applied to the surface.

Weaving

Various weaving techniques can be employed to create or enhance paper surfaces and structures. Look at cloth and braid weaving or basketry for ideas to try out or adapt. Approach it experimentally. The woven element doesn't have to be regular or form the entire structure and other materials can be combined with paper.

- Wrap a small loom or frame with yarn, paper, thread or wire and weave with strips of paper. Experiment with different types of paper. Use cut, torn, thick, thin, twisted, plaited or woven strips and weave evenly, unevenly, create loops or leave gaps and try any other variations you can think of. Remove the weaving from the loom or frame. Stabilise with iron-on interfacing if you wish and enrich with hand or machine stitch or apply to another surface.
- Cut slots in a sheet of paper or paper object and weave with cut or torn strips of paper, metal shim, wire, etc.
- Make a small weaving using wire for the warp, manipulate it into a pleasing shape and dip it in a vat containing pulp with fabric and thread snippets.

Card loom back

Card loom front

Card loom woven

Paper cut, torn and woven

Various woven paper ideas

Paper squares with slots cut, woven together

Paper cut, folded and woven

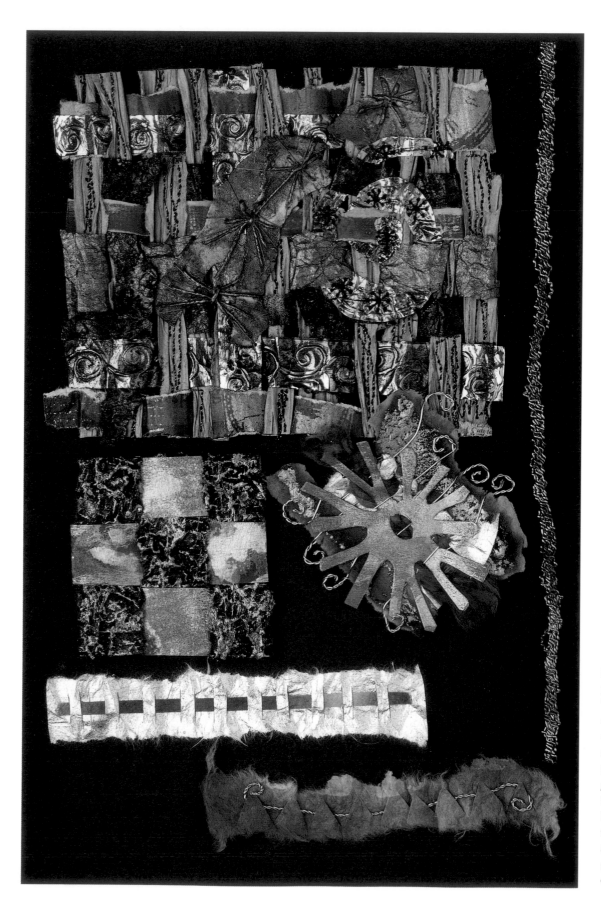

Examples of woven paper including:

Top: paper and embossed copper shim woven and machine stitched to Kunin (acrylic) felt with fragments of *papier mâché* applied by hand.

Middle: copper wire wrapped around a frame and woven with various papers. The wires were cut and twisted together.

Combining techniques

Cover a wire frame with yarn, twine or string. Weave, wrap or work a design in needle-lace or macramé, leaving some areas open. Mix some pulp to a pouring consistency with water and PVA, then add metal leaf flakes, glitter, sequins, etc. Place the frame over a plastic container and pour the mixture over it carefully, building up some areas and allowing the underlying structure to show in others. While the pulp is wet, the surface can be impressed and ink, silk paints or water-colour paint dropped onto the surface. Allow to dry before removing from the frame.

Pulp containing glitter and metal leaf flakes was poured over string wrapped unevenly around a metal frame. Brown ink was dripped onto the surface before the pulp dried.

Have a selection of textured paper, bits of lace and perle thread in different weights (don't worry about colour). Draw a pattern or design on a piece of brown (Kraft) paper, crumple it then reinforce it with iron-on interfacing. Take long straight stitches, by hand, to pick out the main design lines in the heaviest-weight perle. Don't try to follow the lines exactly but use them as a guide and interpret the design loosely. Add detail with lighter-weight threads and apply pieces of torn lace or textured paper to create areas of interest. Remember to leave some quiet areas to balance the design. Cover the surface with gesso and follow with a coat of acrylic paint. Then apply gilding wax or metal leaf and patinate, glaze, distress, etc. or try any of the decorative techniques from the previous chapter.

Use a textured mould or master to make a *papier mâché* vessel or small panel and either tear away one or more sections (to rejoin later) or leave the object whole. Place a sheet of Mulberry tissue on the mould or master and take several small rubbings. Tear the tissue to separate the rubbings, then reinforce with another piece of tissue. Select threads with a pronounced twist or slight texture and stitch, using the rubbings as a guide. The thread on both sides of the stitches will show when the tissue is adhered to another surface, so choose from running, whipped running, Holbein (double running), etc. stitches and avoid trailing threads or knots unless you want them to show.

Left: A design worked on crumpled brown paper in running and fly stitches with torn lace applied.

Right: The surface was sealed with gesso and painted with burnt umber acrylic. Copper wax was applied and left to dry. Black patinating wax and blue moods wax (Liberon products) were used to enrich the effect. Finally, copper was used to add highlights.

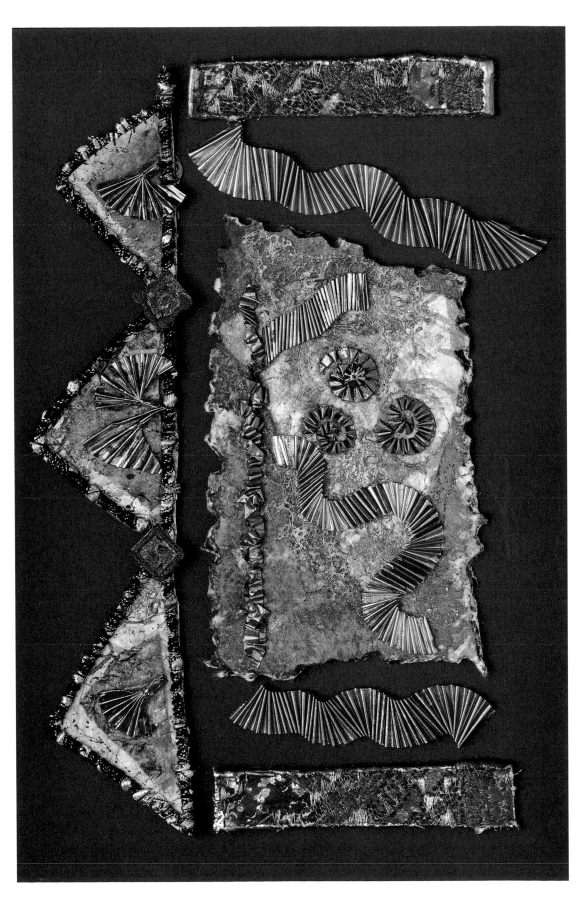

Sampler showing the use of a paper crinkler. Thin strips were curled and wider strips bent into curves with some beading. Some small pieces have been pinched into fan shapes. Cutting the strips with scissors made interesting edges.

More ideas for using the paper crinkler. Some pieces have been pinched into small fan-shaped tassels. These could be made into brooches.

Right: Border taken from the Madonna Icon on page 69. The detail shows a stitched strip of metal with a built in pattern used to provide some detail. Coiled wire was made into heart shapes with beads at the point of the heart. Roundels of stitched shim show the effect of the patination fluids.

Opposite above: Copper blanks (left) were decorated using spirit dyes and embossing powders (right). Some of the embossed ones had stamps pressed into them while the embossing powder was hot.

Opposite below: This detail of a vessel by Rachel Catlow shows glass pieces, as used by florists, trapped inside wire cages. Rachel's clever idea could be used in a variety of ways.

Working with thicker metal

Thicker metals cannot be stitched in the same way as the shim. They can, however, be cut out to make domes or strips. These heavier shapes are great to provide a change of scale and weight. Strips of heavier metal can be cut with tin snips and coiled like the wire.

Copper blanks

What are copper blanks? They are shaped pieces of thicker copper, about 0.66 mm. Craft workers who enamel copper in kilns often use these copper shapes as a basis for their enamelling process. They can be quite useful for us as well, although they are usually much too thick to manipulate or shape. They come in interesting shapes and sizes and it is well worth keeping your eyes open for them. You can often find them in craft shops.

First of all, decorate the copper blanks. This can be by any of the methods described in Chapter 6. They work particularly well with embossing powders and stamped images.

When decorated and completely dry, wrap with a reasonably heavy wire to secure the shape. If you are attaching one of the domes or beaten shapes discussed below, you may find that you need to wrap the wire in two directions and secure the middle with a stitch. See diagram to the left for an explanation.

In fact, it can be very interesting to work buttonhole stitch over the wires to add a stitched element to the metal. Whichever way you decide to do it, make sure your shape is very firmly enclosed in the wire cage and won't come out. Then just stitch in place through the wire, stab stitching to your background going up and down around the edge of the shape, into the wire and down the other side. An alternative to the wire would be to drill the shapes.

Wire wrapped around copper blank

The blanks shown in the photograph on page 83 were wrapped with wire and stitched to a background of distressed velvet. Some shell fragments were applied in the same way.

Sampler

Consolidate all that you have learned in this chapter by making a small sampler. Choose an interesting background fabric, maybe velvet, paper or painted silk. Place the background fabric on a heavy craft Vilene background, using Bondaweb (fusible webbing) or a temporary adhesive spray to hold it in place. Cut shapes from the heat-coloured, embossed metal and arrange them on the fabric. When you are happy with the arrangement, spray the back of the first piece of metal with the temporary adhesive. This will hold it for long enough for you to apply the shape. Spray the shapes one at a time as you stitch them. Add strips of crinkled metal or coiled wire. Think about the edges: turn them under, burn them or use plaited, crinkled strips as a border.

Sampler with Fish: 18 x 26 cm (7 x 10 in). This embroidery used many of the techniques shown so far in the book. The background was hand-made paper. A shaped piece of metal was crinkled using the paper crinkler, and leaves and fish shapes were used in the design, which flows with the paper.

Glass paints

It is quite possible to use glass paints or nail varnish on metal shim. They come in wonderful bright colours and the shine of the metal through the paint can give quite an exciting, extraordinary finish. There are many varieties of glass paint but the one I like best is a bit like painting with warm jelly.

It is best to paint all over a surface, perhaps heating the metal to colour it first. Apply the glass paints using a sponge, allowing the colours to run into each other. Give them a good long time to dry. Paint the metal first and then draw any embossing designs into it afterwards. The effects of the paints merging together with the lines running through to join them can be quite extraordinary and well worth pursuing. Stitching must be done a long, long time after the paint has dried, so allow some time for this technique. Give it a good week to dry before stitching into the surface.

You can also use these paints on the embossed, acrylic wiped, designs. Paint in the specific areas and allow to dry. Then rub with a little wax to soften the effect.

This detail, which forms a decorative panel on a book, shows the exciting results that can be achieved using glass paints and nail varnish. The rectangles of shim were stitched to paper with a central area of woven strips. The metal was painted after stitching.

Another glass painting material is called Pebeo (Crystal) Gel. These are lovely, translucent gels which come in many colours and are particularly good with metal. Build up in thin layers by painting the gel all over one piece of metal, then put another piece of metal on top and pull it away. You will be left with a very 'organic' pattern. When dry, repeat with another colour. These gels aren't as obvious as the glass paints or as brightly coloured, but they can have a very subtle gleam of their own, especially when the metal underneath is coloured and this shows through.

Using embossing powders with metal

Embossing powders are generally used by rubber stampers to raise their designs above the surface. They can be very effective on metal provided that a 'sticking agent' ensures that the embossing powder sticks to the metal. The sticking agent could be a wax, a paint that can be heated, or Pebeo (Crystal) Gel.

Wax

Just rub the wax quite heavily over the metal, and sprinkle lightly with embossing powder. Shake off any remnants onto a piece of paper (they can go back into the embossing powder pot). Then use a heat tool to raise the areas of embossing powder. You will find that you can create different effects depending upon how thickly you sprinkle the powder.

Paints and gels

Embossing powders can also be used over paint as long as it is safe to heat. It is worth finding out (don't try it with anything you are not sure about) – the Stewart Gill range are advertised as being suitable. Pebeo Gels, as discussed on the previous page, are particularly safe as they are designed to go into the oven. Just dab or brush on the Pebeo Gel, sprinkle over the embossing powder, shake it off and heat it, as before.

Stamps

It is quite possible to use rubber stamps or wooden blocks to put motif designs on metal. For this, brush the Pebeo Gel onto a thick piece of polythene or glass so that you have a surface pool to dip the stamp into. Then place your stamp, face down, in the Pebeo Gel and transfer it by placing it carefully (just tap it down) on the metal. Lift it off cleanly, cover with the embossing powder, shake off the excess and heat as you did before. You will find

This piece of brass shim was first stitched, then wax was applied and embossing powders were shaken over the stitching and heated. After this, the piece was given a further coating of wax and Pearl Ex powders.

that the stamp has created an interesting surface on top of the metal. Alternatively, heat several layers of embossing powder by shaking more powder on after heating and then push an inked stamp into it. This will give a deep impression.

Try adding effects like wax with coloured Pearl Ex powders or black patinating wax over the top of the stamped image, to add definition.

A moulding mat was used on this metal, stamped with black 'Staz-on' (designed for difficult surfaces) ink. The top piece shows what happens if you then use embossing powder and press the stamp into it. The middle and lower ones show the effect of just the stamp with the ink and some slight crinkling and stitching. Wrapped pipe cleaners add interest.

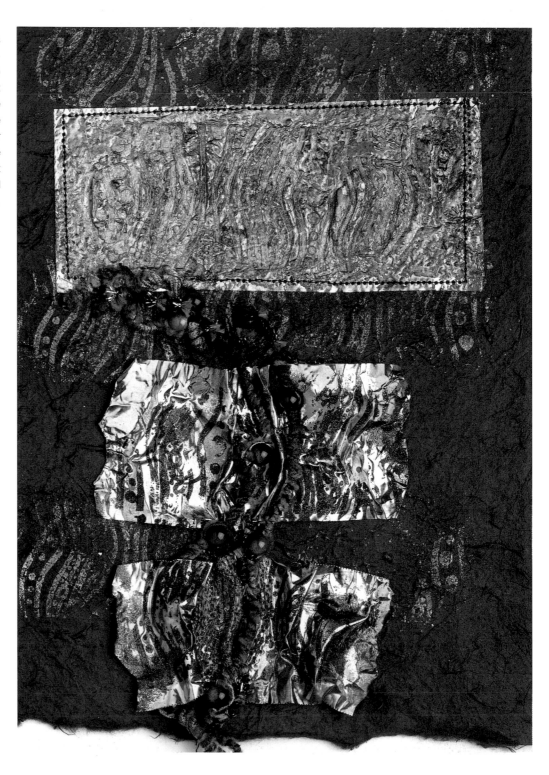

Decorating the metal with Lazertran

Lazertran is a paper product. You take your image and a sheet of Lazertran to the photocopy shop where they copy your image onto the paper using their *laser colour copier* (it doesn't work with a black-and-white copier, even if the image is black-and-white – and it may damage the copier). It is almost impossible to do this at home, even with a laser printer. It just won't work. There are particular photocopiers that it works with (it tells you this on the packet). Although this makes it an expensive medium, it is really the best way of transferring your image onto metal.

This diagram shows suitable designs for placing on shim using the Lazertran transfer method. Sometimes the outlines are lost when the design is placed onto the metal and you will note that on the figures, the outline has been exaggerated using an ordinary ballpoint pen.

You can see here the Lazertran process. Top left is the original design on paper. Top right is the design transferred to Lazertran and floated off onto the metal. The two little photos bottom left show what happens when this is heated, and the piece on the right shows a small embroidery made using the Lazertran.

Float the Lazertran off in water (just like a children's transfer), place it on the metal and dab gently with a kitchen towel until all the water has come out of it. Leave it overnight to allow it to dry thoroughly. When that's done, heat it, either with an iron or a heat tool, or put it in the oven, and the plastic coating disappears, leaving the toner to colour the metal. So it's not a surface technique but it actually lays colour right into the metal.

It is possible to use any design, such as a photograph, computer image or a drawing from your sketchbook. If you use an image from a book, make sure that it is copyright free. Don't take anybody else's work – it's just not worth it.

It is well worth colouring the metal with heat first. This adds a lot of interest as you see the metal coming through the colours of the Lazertran.

There are certain things to bear in mind when using Lazertran. For instance, any areas that are without colour in the original image will become completely transparent and just show the colour of the metal. Some colours, if they are metal-coloured (oranges and, to some extent, yellows), might be absorbed and will not show up well. A dark, well-defined image comes through the best. Some of the images shown on page 95 will give you an idea of the results.

To use Lazertran successfully:

1   Cut out the design copied onto Lazertran and float it in a bowl of water. Take it out and, very carefully, check that the top plastic is sliding off the backing paper.

2   Lift it off, lay it onto your metal, dab very, very gently with a paper towel and then leave it completely alone overnight. If you don't allow the time, you will find there is water trapped underneath and, when you apply heat, it will make bubbles in the plastic that will pop. Sometimes, of course, this makes an exciting image and you might like the effect of the popped bubble, so it's well worth trying a piece to see what happens.

3   Now follow the pack instructions for heating. Either heat in an oven (preferably not one you cook food in) or place it on a heat-resistant surface and use a heat tool until the metal becomes shiny and scratching the image does not affect the colour. Be careful when picking it up – allow it time to cool.

4   When you have heated it and the plastic has all disappeared, you can then consider taking it through to stitch as described in Chapter 7.

One thing that you might consider is combining a Lazertraned image (when the Lazertran has been heated and firmly set on the metal) with any of the above methods for colouring metal. For instance, using the shellac and paint method, you could just paint some areas of the image as though a verdigris effect has started but has not completely covered the image. This could give interesting effects. The glass paints also work particularly well, carefully painted over part of the image.

I have used Lazertran to put a series of icon images from my sketchbook on metal. As it can be used on any surface it is possible to place complementary designs on the frame used with the embroidery, linking the two together.

7
Into Stitch with Metal

We covered the very basic elements of stitching into metal in Chapter 5. If you always remember to have a weighty fabric as a base for the metal (and craft Vilene is ideal for this), you will be able to stitch without constant thread breaks. For happy stitching, make sure that the thickness of the metal is not greater than 0.05 mm. The copper is easier to work into than the brass for stitching as it is softer. Copper can always be heated to produce a gold colour if that is needed. Metal can be used in embroidery in so many ways. Small pieces can be used to add accents or larger, embossed areas could form the main focus of the work. Lazertran can be used for detailed images, such as the icon shown below.

One of the main advantages of stitching into the metal is that the stitching automatically knocks back the shine. This is one of the results that we are aiming for. In this chapter, we look at stitching on different surfaces, adding wires and manipulated metal pieces and making borders and patches to build up embroideries.

Dark Matter Angel 2: 23 x 33 cm (9 x 13 in). This Icon image was transferred using Lazertran. The background fabric is craft Vilene bonded with tissue paper. A cut-out border runs along the left of the piece and small patches were applied to provide a finishing touch.

Opposite: *Coffee Grid*: 92 x 122 cm (36 x 54 in) by Anna Nowicki (detail). This embroidery has a waxed and varnished paper background. Further paper, in a distressed grid, was applied and the whole embellished with small boxes made from heated aluminium drinks cans. In some areas the machine was used without thread to make marks.

Metal with water-soluble paper

Water-soluble (dissolvable) paper can be tricky to work with but has such possibilities that it is worth making an effort to master it. In particular, it can be used with metal shim to give the effect of rusting, degraded artefacts and it is possible to make lighter, lacier edgings with the paper.

It works like this:

1   Colour the metal with heat and draw lines with the embossing tool, if required. Place the metal on craft Vilene cut to the same size. Using the water-soluble paper double, cut into strips to be placed over the metal; top and bottom gives good edges. Brush out some puff paint (Xpandaprint) onto glass or plastic and use a stamp or block to decorate some areas of the paper. *Do not heat the paint yet.* Then lay the paper over the metal shim so that it overlaps the edge.

2   Use free running stitch to attach the paper to the metal. This stitching will not show too much in the final piece. Change the foot and work some random built-in patterns. They should look like part of an old design that has become eroded. After stitching use a heat tool or an iron to puff the paint.

Carved Bark: 30 x 18 cm (12 x 7 in). A heavily embossed piece of metal is the focal point for this work. This was applied to painted, tissued Vilene and then areas of the Vilene were cut away. Pieces of water-soluble fabric were stitched over the cut outs. Shim was then stitched to the edges of the Vilene and embossed before being coloured with waxes and Pearl Ex powders. Finally, an interesting shape was achieved by bending the metal edges.

3 Now use nail varnish or Pebeo (Crystal) Gel as a resist on some areas of the water-soluble paper. Don't use too much – the effect you want is a lacy, fragmented, distressed effect on the metal. You can see where it is used in the photo below.

4 When the nail varnish or Pebeo Gel is dry, pin it all to a sheet of polystyrene and very, very carefully, with a paintbrush, add water. Just have a bowl of cold water to hand and splash with your paintbrush. You will find that areas of the paper that aren't resisted will turn into soggy mounds. This is to be encouraged. Move the soggy mounds around with the brush, especially over the metal. Make sure that the edges are particularly light and delicate.

5 When you have finished this, dab it very gently with a paper towel and then allow it to dry. It needs to be completely dry. When it is, paint it, either with a metal paint or with an acrylic.

6 When the painting is finished and dry, apply metallic wax and lustre powders to both surfaces so that you have integrated them to look like the same piece of work. Any of the finishes in Chapter 6 will work. If you have used metal paints, the patination fluids, including rust, can be used. Spirit-soluble dyes look great, too. You should have an effect similar to that in the photo below.

Water-soluble paper can be an interesting surface when placed on the metal. The steps are shown here. First the paper was stamped with Xpandaprint and lightly stitched. The paper was then heated so that the Xpandaprint puffed. The next step was to apply a resist – in this case nail varnish. Then, water was very gently splashed on, to dissolve the paper. Not all the paper was dissolved. As you can see, this stage looks a bit messy but the last two stages show the effect of painting and waxing this surface.

Applying fabrics to metal

Metal Flora: 30 x 18 cm (12 x 7 in).
Embroidery with water-soluble paper.
The method shown in the previous
photograph has been employed
here. You can see how exciting the
gleam of the metal is when it comes
through the paper. The stitching is
just visible in this piece of work.

Interesting effects can be obtained by stitching fabric onto the metal, rather than the other
way round. This is even more interesting if the metal is stitched first. Start by taking some
coloured metal shim. Use any of the ideas in Chapter 6. Place on craft Vilene and work
bands of stitching. Then try placing strips of fabric, or stitched water-soluble paper, over the
top and using free running stitch to secure and add texture. Work small samples to get the
feel of the technique.

Here are some ideas.

- Bond sheer fabric to metal and then zap with a heat tool. Try stitching the fabric first.
- Stitch some Kunin (acrylic) felt to the metal. Zap with a heat tool after stitching. This looks good when cut into shapes, too.
- Cut up some space-dyed velvet – the fine, acrylic variety. Place strips on the metal and stitch. Use free running stitch and work in small circles to make the most of the texture.

Gilded Lace: 15 x 36 cm (6 x 14 in). Here metal forms an underlying base for a series of applied fabrics. Painted lace motifs, cut out pieces of built-in patterns and nets, with some embossing powder applied to them, were all stitched on to the metal in this embroidery. The metal gleams through but the shine was knocked back. Machine-wrapped cords made a finishing touch.

A piece of water-soluble fabric over metal is used for this book cover. The fabric was designed and stitched first, then laid over the shim. Embossing tools were used to draw a pattern around the edges and into the gaps in the water-soluble piece of stitching. After stitching the water soluble piece, the metal was coloured using acrylic paints. The spine shows braids stitched, with strips of metal cut out with a paper punch.

- Apply scraps of painted lace. Stitch them to the metal, working around the pattern on the lace. Brush on some Pebeo (Crystal) Gel paint and sprinkle with embossing powder. Heat until it bubbles. If you have a purpose-made Melting-Pot (see page 112), melt the thick embossing powder in that and pour it over the lace.
- Stitch built-in patterns or heavy machine embroidery on felt or painted craft Vilene. Cut it out close to the stitching and then place on the metal and stitch around the edge to integrate it.
- Make some embossed fragments from paper pulp as described on page 24. Paint these and apply to the metal with lots of stitching to blend in.
- Try free machining a design on water-soluble fabric. Make sure you lock the stitches by working several lines of stitch over each other. Dissolve the fabric and apply to previously embossed and colour-heated metal. Apply the water-soluble fragment by hand or machine.

Borders

Metal is particularly effective for making borders. For inspiration, look at the wonderful illuminated manuscripts such as the Lindisfarne Gospels or the Book of Kells. Some of the pages are almost entirely composed of borders, interspersed with roundels or motifs. The borders described here can be used with an embossed centre or a Lazertran image as the main centre of interest. They could also be used with the patches described in the next section.

A good technique that you might try is to work strips of built-in machine stitches using a variegated thread on the metal shim or Wiremesh, which could be coloured with heat before making the border. Make sure that the thread you choose has good colour contrasts as these will show up as you stitch. It is easier to stitch the strips on a larger piece of Vilene and cut them out after stitching. Work as follows.

This drawing is based on one of the wonderful pages in the Book of Kells. You will note how this is composed of long borders and other areas that could be patches. On page 115, you can see a partly stitched version of this design.

Here are some samples that could be made into borders. The strips of metal or Wiremesh have been heavily stitched with built in patterns using variegated threads. The thread used was wound on card and is shown with its relevant strip so that you can see how the colours work. The strip at the bottom was stitched on Wiremesh, which was later burned to give an ancient and tatty look. These would just need edging to make wonderful borders.

1 Cut a piece of heavy Vilene about 15 x 20 cm (6 x 8 in).

2 Cut out a piece of black fabric such as cotton or polycotton and lay it over the Vilene before stitching. Place strips of metal about 2.5 cm (1 in) across on top of this. The black fabric will stop the holes in the metal made by the needle from showing white. It also gives a more dramatic effect.

3 Now machine across the band of metal with a variegated thread using a built-in stitch pattern. The stitches can follow a pattern or form random lines. Remember the difference that stitch direction and thread colour can make. In the photo below the thread is shown alongside each piece, so you can get an idea of the way the colour changes.

These pieces make wonderful borders and, as you can see, the stitching is knocking-back the shine. If you are feeling brave, try stitching on Wiremesh and burning the stitching with a candle. Do this outside with a bowl of water handy and put out any flames by covering immediately with a heavy, damp cloth or dunking in the bucket. When dry, iron interfacing on the back to prevent the stitching from unravelling.

An alternative to the metal border is to use the tissue/Vilene background with metal cut-outs free-machined along the length. Or use this background with metallic embossing powder and a rubber stamp with an intricate design for an all-over border pattern.

Both types of border benefit from applied wire shapes, perhaps with beads. The borders can be used as long strips or cut into sections. The next step is to edge the strips.

A variety of borders are shown here with wire, small pieces of metal, cut out stitching and frayed cable wires applied to them. Note how the borders have been edged. Buttonhole stitch, dimension paint, embossing powders and cut strips of Vilene were all used.

Border edges

The edges of the borders will probably need to be finished in some way. There are several methods for doing this.

- Cut strips of tea-dyed craft Vilene to make a narrow border all around the metal strip. Put in place and stitch down using a narrow built-in stitch pattern.
- Embossing powder could be used. Just paint the edges of the strip with Pebeo Gel and dip them into some powder shaken onto a sheet of paper. When well coated, heat them with a heat tool to puff them up. An alternative to this method is to purchase a Melting-Pot, a wonderful invention that heats and melts embossing powder. When the powder is melted, the border or tile can be dipped into the pot, using tongs or tweezers.
- Dimensional paint can make neat edges. Just pipe the paint along the edge of the border and place on baking parchment to set.
- Wrap pipe-cleaners with textured yarn and bend them around the edge. Couch them down by hand. Fancy stitches could be used here.
- Buttonhole stitches could be worked by hand around the edge.

Patches

Patches are small pieces of embroidery. They can be applied as design elements in a variety of shapes to enhance a focal point. In some cases a large patch could form the focal point.

Some of the design ideas for making patches. You will have plenty of ideas of your own for these.

A good background to make patches is tissue paper bonded to felt or craft Vilene to make a fabric. This is then either tea-dyed or painted and a little metallic wax is used to add a gleam. This base is cut up into the appropriate shapes and further fabrics or metals applied to it. These could include some of the following.

Right: Samples of patches are shown here. There are many different ways of making these patches. Most of these show a base of tissue paper on Vilene, suitably cut-out. Small pieces of Xpandaprint were painted and applied, and some metal and wires were also used.

- Black Xpandaprint or puff paint can make interesting small tiles to stitch onto a patch. The paint can be placed in a squeezy container with a nozzle that gives thin lines of piping. These are often used for gutta with silk paint. Pipe out some shapes, like the ones shown in the diagram overleaf, onto craft Vilene. Then scatter some embossing powder over the top (there are some available that look very antique), shake off the excess and puff the paint. Take care not to burn the craft Vilene. Paint with any permanent medium – silk paints or acrylics – and cut out the individual pieces to stitch onto the patches.

This is one of the components of patches that can be very useful. Black Xpandaprint is placed in a bottle with a nozzle and then piped into shapes on craft Vilene. Another way to do this is to use a cocktail stick, dip it into the Xpandaprint and use that for making the longer lines. The shapes were painted after puffing.

Small designs like these work well to make the Xpandaprint pieces ready to apply.

- Strips of metal or Wiremesh could be cut and stitched to the patch.
- Rubber-stamped images could be used, either on their own or with embossing powder.
- Small pieces of metal could be shaped in the paper crinkler and applied.
- Little tiles could be made of embossed metal, used plain, or coloured by any of the methods described in Chapter 6.
- Heavier metal could be applied, such as domes or curled strips.
- The Melting-Pot can be used to great effect. Small pieces of net or lace could be dipped into it and stitched to the patch. Better still, try small pieces of embroidery – a good use for a piece of work that 'went wrong'. Or the embossing powder could be drizzled from the Melting-Pot onto the patch and beads set into it. There are so many opportunities with this gadget.

There are, of course, many more ways of stitching the metal and you will be sure to have some ideas of your own. In Chapter 8 we consider ways of putting all these stitch techniques together to make completed textiles.

This shows the Kells design from page 109 partly stitched. You can see some of the borders and patches already stitched in place. The paper design was cut out and placed on a dark fabric to give ideas of where the next pieces will go. You will find that the design changes as you stitch, but it is a good idea to make a pattern to give yourself an initial idea for the placement and to see how the shapes work together.

8

Putting it All Together

We have looked at different ways of inscribing, decorating, colouring and stitching metal and you should have some plans of your own for combining all the elements in your textiles. Some ideas are described here but don't copy them slavishly – use them as a base from which to launch your own work. Using a variety of borders and patches will help to combine the techniques.

Icons and manuscripts

Tremendous inspiration can be gained from illuminated manuscripts or some of the wonderful historic icons. These lend themselves in particular to the metal treatment, especially when Lazertran is brought in for the main images. Try to trace, copy or draw and paint the design yourself as there may be copyright issues in photocopying from a book. Emphasise the outlines before copying onto the Lazertran as they may fade a little in the transfer. The following is the method of construction.

First make a background – this method is suitable for both icons and manuscripts.

1   Cut a piece of craft Vilene to the size required and then cut a piece of Bondaweb (fusible webbing) to that size and a piece of tissue paper slightly larger.
    If you have a computer and inkjet printer, you may want to print onto the tissue paper before using it, especially with manuscripts where you might use a word processor to type random words or phrases to be printed on your tissue paper. The way to do this is as follows.

    a Cut a piece of tissue paper to A4 size and then apply a gluestick firmly around the edges of a piece of ordinary A4 printing paper, photocopy paper or whatever you use in your printer.

    b Press the tissue onto the glued paper, making sure that all the edges are covered with tissue paper and very firmly stuck. This should go through an inkjet printer without any problem. (It is not advisable to use this method on a laser printer.)

    c Put this sheet through the printer to get your words onto it and then release the tissue paper by cutting or pulling it away from the glued edges.

If you don't have access to a computer, try to find a rubber stamp with lettering – there are lots about. Stamp with black or brown ink and try for a distressed look, as shown overleaf. Or try copying some manuscript-type writing or calligraphy. Whichever method you use, allow the paper to dry overnight. You are now ready for the second step.

2   Crumple the tissue gently, then iron the Bondaweb (fusible webbing) onto the craft Vilene, making sure it is very well stuck. Now pull the paper from the Bondaweb. While the Bondaweb is still warm, put your crumpled tissue paper on top of it, adding a few extra crumples as you lay it down. When you are satisfied, iron it well again through baking parchment.

Flat Plan for a Landscape: 30 x 60 cm (12 x 24 in). The idea for this embroidery was based on the page plans used by editors and writers, which are usually bristling with Post-it notes. When God was in planning mode, I had an idea that his might look a little like this. The centre is a tissue paper design with raised areas of Lazertraned metal. This represents the boiling earth. The little notes around the edges are all patches, which say things like 'No Fishing' and 'Grass and Trees Go Here'.

You can see here an icon piece under construction. Stitching has begun on the metal which was Lazertranned with an angel design from a sketch book. In this case, the lettering was drawn (and smudged) directly onto a tea-dyed and webbing-sprayed background.

3   You can now dab the tissue paper with teabags. Tea-dyeing gives a very satisfying aged-manuscript look to a piece. Pour a very little amount of boiling water over the teabags. This can be adjusted to get the colour you require. If you want to add more colour, you can put a spot or two of silk paint onto your teabag and use that while dabbing. Use it sparingly though; you don't want large areas of colour. The background should be quite neutral on these pieces.

4 Now let the background dry completely. To distress the lettering, stitch over a
piece of tea-dyed nappy (diaper) liner, fine agricultural fleece, Sizoflor or
Thermogauze vanishing muslin. Rub with a Markal (Shiva) oilstick and zap with a
heat tool. Finally, rub on a very little wax, which can be Liberon or Treasure
Gold. Rub very, very lightly, just highlighting a few creases. You may wish, before
applying the wax, to add a squirt of black webbing spray, which gives a darker
look. Sometimes these pieces with the tea-dye can be too tonally similar (all one
colour), so a little bit of the dark webbing spray works wonders. Make sure you
do it *before* you apply the wax, or it won't stick.

This shows three ways of
distressing stamped, lettered
backgrounds to give an aged look.
The top is Thermogauze, the
middle is nappy liner and the
bottom shows Sizoflor – all zapped
after stitching.

Designs for icon embroidery

You now have a background ready for you to make up into either a manuscript piece or an icon. We will look at the icon piece first.

1   From your sketchbook, choose a suitable icon image and copy it onto Lazertran. Float it off the Lazertran, as described on page 95, and put it onto the metal. When completely dry, heat with a heat tool to merge the Lazertran image completely with the metal.

2   Now place the image in a suitable position on your background. This will obviously be the focal point of the work. Look at books containing images of icons; they will give you lots of ideas. It really is worth spending a little time on the design of these pieces. Just sketch out some rough elements of the design first; then you won't be working completely in the dark.

3   When you are happy with the placement of the metal on the background, it's time to begin stitching. Using one of the temporary adhesives will help to hold the metal in place. Use stitch or embossing powders on the image and then wax on top of that to knock back the shine.

4   When you have done that, consider how you might make borders around this particular part of the design. Perhaps stitch some built-in patterns onto black felt, cut them out and stitch them over the top of the metalled image. When you are completely happy with this part of the design, move onto other design elements. Some of the shaped patches would work well.

5   You will have prepared these patches in advance. Consider that they might be shapes cut out in metal and perhaps stitched onto another piece of tissue bonded to craft Vilene, and free machined. Or they could be strips of such designs with borders made from built-in stitch patterns. Consider all these elements first.

6   Other things that work well can be to added to the design. These could include raised domes or some of the heavy metal strips curled into shapes. Use free running stitch to attach the patches to the background.

7 When your icon piece is complete, consider how you might frame it. They can be most effective framed straight onto a piece of medium density fibreboard (MDF). The embroidery can be firmly glued to the fibreboard with contact adhesive and the edges of the board could have strips of tea-dyed tissue on Vilene glued to them. With care, it is possible to oversew or buttonhole the edges.

Manuscript pieces can be worked in much the same way. Have a look at some of the Celtic or Anglo-Saxon manuscripts, and try taking a single element, exaggerating the size and working into it with stitching and then framing it with lots of little border pieces. If you look at something like the Lindisfarne Gospels, you will find that they are incredibly well constructed with design elements placed in long borders.

These pieces can be constructed in exactly the same way as the icon pieces.

Alternatives for patches

Sometimes just one large patch works well (see below). Alternatively, find ways of integrating a tissue print with Lazertran on metal. A computer design could be used and printed on tissue as described on page 116, or the tissue could be painted, inked and bleached, or otherwise decorated. An abstract design is best. Here is the method.

1   Bond colourful decorated tissue to craft Vilene. Paint and wax if necessary.

2   Take this piece to the copy shop and have the design photocopied onto Lazertran. Float the Lazertran onto metal and heat it to transfer the toner.

3   Cut the coloured metal into shapes that will fit well with the design. Move them around to get the best design. If you want the metal to be slightly raised then back the cut-out shapes with felt.

4   Stitch the metal to the tissue piece. If using felt, stitch around the shape and then cut away the excess. Stitch the edges again to integrate (see the effect on page 117).

5   Make patches to enhance the design. These could be placed around the edges as a border or become an integral part of the design. Attach by hand or with free running stitch. The diagrams (right) show some ideas.

The Sky Shivers: 30 x 50 cm (12 x 20 in). Tissue paper on Vilene was painted and then lines from a poem about winter were written by hand. A large patch with metal and Xpandaprint pieces was applied together with pieces of Japanese paper, painted and waxed.

Right: Ideas for using patches as frames.

Weaving techniques with paper and metal

Metal can work very well combined with strips of stitched paper to give a woven effect. Shaped pieces of metal could form a central point or be placed to one side. The metal will probably form the centre of interest so be aware of this when planning your squares.

Metallic Weave: 30 x 30 cm (12 x 12 in). This shows a woven embroidery using the paper strip method with stamped images. The strips were coloured with inks and decorated with foil. Note the heavily embossed squares of metal that lift and enhance the design.

First of all, emboss your metal and colour it as you wish. A small motif is ideal for this. The shapes could be squares, triangles or rectangles. For this technique these seem to work better than amorphous shapes. The metal can be coloured in any way you choose, but obviously the colour of the strips will influence this.

Now for the woven strips. It is possible to use fabric but paper is especially easy to work with as you don't have to worry about the edges. If you use a fabric, you must finish the edges in some way. Burning, overstitching or something similar, or using a product like Fraycheck, will stop the edges wearing away. Be aware when weaving strips that the edges rub together, so it needs to be a fairly permanent solution.

Opposite: *Knight and his Lady* (height 40 cm/16 in). These delightful figures were made by Chris Hardy using the paper weaving method. She varied the size of the strips to make them thinner for the limbs and larger for the body. They have faces and hearts made from embossed metal.

You could try handmade paper, painted in bright colours. Stamp over the top with rubber stamps or Rollagraphs (these are stamps on a roller which work really well here). Use clear embossing fluid and clear powder. Heat with a heat tool. Now iron some transfer foil over the top. Try to use an old piece of foil so that the metallic effect is not too heavy. Then paint with black or coloured ink. The embossing powder will resist the ink and allow the colour underneath to show through. If you use a bleach-reactive ink then try bleaching on top for extra interest. Cut into strips of suitable size. Stitch if required. Built-in stitch patterns work well. Stitch onto black felt to thicken the strips. Trim the felt close to the edges.

When you have done all this and prepared your strips and your metal pieces, cut a piece of Vilene to the size of the finished piece. You may be making a piece to stand in its own right, or maybe a 'quilt' where you piece all your weavings together afterwards. Whichever technique you use, you will need to cut the Vilene to size.

Use your strips to build up the shape. This could be traditional weaving with the strips running in and out of each other and the metal placed as required, or perhaps a log-cabin effect around the piece of metal. Whichever you want to do, make sure that the strips surround the metal and are firmly held together. Pin them firmly to the Vilene to hold in place as you weave.

Then try some stitching. This could be almost invisible, with just stab stitching from the back to hold the strips down, or quite heavy machine embroidery which could be worked over the weaving to hold it in place. Fold the ends of the strips over to the back and secure to finish.

As you can see, there are many ways of combining the metal with paper, fabric, wire and other media. Do give them all a try, carry out lots of experiments – and have fun along the way.

Opposite: A delicate embroidery (15 x 20 cm/ 6 x 8 in) by Sue Miles using metal and paper strips woven with razor shells. The shells were stamped with lettering and the base is tea-dyed tissue and Vilene. The colours are sympathetic to the shells and enhance them.

Below: Ready to weave strips.

Resources and Bibliography

Sewing machines
Bernina, Bogod Machine Company, 50–52 Great Sutton Street, London EC1V 0DJ

Brother, Shepley Street, Guide Bridge, Audenshaw, Manchester M34 5JD

Husqvarna/Pfaff, Husqvarna/Viking House, Cheddar Business Park, Wedmore Road, Cheddar, Somerset BS27 3EB

Janome, Janome Centre, Southside, Bredbury, Stockport, Cheshire SK6 2SP

Equipment and materials
The following suppliers have a mail order service and will send you a catalogue.

Art Van Go, The Studios, 1 Stevenage Road, Knebworth, Hertfordshire SG3 6AN
email: art@artvango.co.uk
(bronze powders, glass paints, Lazertran, metallic wax, paper and papermaking supplies, paper crinkler, patination fluids, shellac, Transfoil, Treasure Gold, Webbing Spray, Wireform, Wiremesh, Xpandaprint, lustre powders, Markal paintsticks, transfer gold, imitation leaf)

Axminster Tools Ltd, FREEPOST SWB 30746, Axminster, Devon EX13 5ZZ
(Spirit-soluble dyes)

June Carroll, 137 Mildmay Road, Chelmsford, Essex CM2 0DT
email: jac@mildmay63.freeserve.co.uk
(Grilon thread)

Falkiner Fine Papers, 76 Southampton Row, London WC1 4AR
tel. 020 7831 1151
(paper)

Stef Francis, Waverley, Higher Rocombe, Stokeinteignhead, Newton Abbot, Devon TQ12 4QL *email*: sales@stef-francis.co.uk
(metal shim, wire)

Stewart Gill, 20 Lochrin Buildings, Edinburgh EH3 9NB
email: enquiries@stewartgill.com
(rubber stamps, paints, embossing powders)

Ivy House Studio, 37 High Street, Kessingland, Suffolk NR33 7QQ
email: ivyhousestudio@hotmail.com
(copper blanks, Melting-Pot, paper crinkler, water-soluble paper, Webbing Spray, surface decoration supplies including embossing powders, mica flakes)

Jackson's Art Supplies, PO Box 29568, London N1 4WT
email: sales@jacksonart.com
(art supplies including gold and imitation leaf, loose and transfer)

Lazertran, 8 Alban Square, Aberaeron, Ceredigion SA46 0LX
email: mic@lazertran.com
(Lazertran)

Oliver Twists, 22 Phoenix Road, Crowther, Washington, Tyne & Wear NE38 0AD
email: jean@olivertwists.freeserve.co.uk
(metal shim, enamelled wire, variegated machine threads, hand-stitch threads)

The Paper Shed, March House, Tollerton, York YO6 2EG,
email: papershed@papershed.com
(paper and paper-making supplies)

John Purcell Paper, 15 Rumsey Road, London SW9 0TR
email: jpp@johnpurcell.net
(paper and paper-making fibres)

Rainbow Silks, 6 Wheelers Yard, High Street, Great Missenden, Buckinghamshire HP16 0AL
email: rainbowsilks@rainbowsilks.co.uk
(embossing powders, Melting-Pot, moulding mats, Mold 'n' Pour, water-soluble paper, surface decoration supplies including Paper-Etch, various metal leaf flakes, Rollagraphs)

Winifred Cottage, 17 Elms Road, Fleet, Hampshire GU13 9EG
email: WinifCott@aol.com
(embossing powders, temporary adhesive [505 spray], Thermogauze, water-soluble paper, Webbing Spray, YLI fusible thread, Sizoflor)

General supplies
Glass paints, Liberon wax, paper cutters, Polymer clay and Pebeo Gel are available from art or hobby shops. Bondaweb is available from haberdashers. You can buy embossing powders from stamp shops.

North America
Most materials in this book are available from art suppliers, but specifically:

American Art Clay Co.
website: www.amaco.com
(Wireform, Wiremesh, shim)

Clearsnap Inc, PO Box98, Anacortes, WA 98221, USA
email: Linda.Brown@clearsnapinc.com
(moulding mats, Rollagraphs)

Embroidery Adventures
email: reliker@embroideryadventures.com
(most embroidery supplies)

Gerber EZ-Liner Diaper Liners,
800-4- GERBER
(diaper liners)

Impress Me
website: www.impressmenow.com
(Impress Me stamps)

Kunin Felt, 380 Lafayete Road, Hamptin, NH 03842, USA. *tel*: 800-292-7900
(zappable felt)

Lazertran, USA
email: lazertran@msn.com

Meinke Toy, PMB#411, 55 E Long Lake Rd, Troy MI 48085, USA
email: info@meinketoy.com
(YLI/Grilon, Thermogauze, Water-soluble paper, puff paint)

Sepp Leaf Products
tel: 212 683 2840
(liberon spirit-soluble dyes)

Australia & New Zealand
The Thread Studio, 6 Smith Street, Perth 6000, Western Australia
tel: +61 (0)9 227 1561
email: dale@thethreadstudio.com
(most supplies)

New Zealand
Craft Supplies, 31 Gurney Road, Belmont, Lower Hutt, New Zealand
(most supplies)

Bibliography

The Art and Craft of Papermaking, Sophie Dawson, Aurum Press 1 85410 363 6

Papermaking for Basketry and other Crafts, ed. Lynn Stearns, Lark Books 0 937274 62 3

Paper-Making-Decorating-Designing, Beata Thackeray, Conran Octopus 1 85029 893 9

On Paper, Jane Thomas and Paul Jackson, Merrell 1 85894 145 8

A basic knowledge of machine embroidery has been assumed for this book. To learn machine embroidery, we recommend:

Machine Embroidery Stitch Techniques, Valerie Campbell-Harding and Pamela Watts, B T Batsford 0 7134 5797 X

Raising the Surface with Machine Embroidery, Maggie Grey, B T Batsford 0 7134 8851 4

The Crafter's Pattern Sourcebook, Mary MacCarthy, Collins & Brown 1 85585 6182
(good for tracing motifs)

Index